How to Start a Business in

SOUTH AFRICA

The Ultimate Guide to Doing Business in South Africa

Looking to Start a Business in South Africa?

For most people, starting their own business is a lifelong dream. For others, the thought comes out of necessity - a job loss or a major life change. No matter the reason you are now at a place in your life where you would like to strike out on your own and start a new business, South Africa is ripe for growth, investment and new businesses. Some of the areas that are seeing the greatest growth include: agriculture, tourism, construction, manufacturing and exporting.

South Africa has trade relationships with many other African countries as well as the United States, the United Kingdom, Germany, China, Japan and Spain.

The country has a growing middle class, abundant resources, a stock market in the top 20 of the world and the infrastructure to move goods throughout the country, the region and the world. South Africa boasts a fairly sophisticated financial framework including communications, legal, transportation and energy sectors.

Why do business in South Africa?

- South Africa is one of the largest economies in Africa, with a GDP per capita of 7575.24 and per capita PPP of 12389.96.

- South Africa is home to three of the most livable cities in the world – Port Elizabeth, Cape Town and Johannesburg.

- South Africa offers ease of access to start a business with very little bureaucracy and red tape.

- South Africa offers beautiful beaches, expansive forests and deserts, a great choice of climates and amazing wildlife.

- The quality of life with great food, good living accommodations and a strong climate for economic growth is better than many places.

In short, South Africa offers everything you would want in an economic climate, quality of life and opportunity. Few countries in the world can offer what South Africa does in terms of world class infrastructure, gorgeous beaches, native wildlife roaming the plains, exciting cities and great weather. It is a great place to start a new business.

CONTENTS

CHAPTER 1

A PRESENTATION OF SOUTH AFRICA FORENTREPRENEURS

General Presentation

Before considering starting a business in South Africa, it is important to know the basics about the country. In this chapter we will share a little about the history and culture of South Africa. We will look at the marketing demographics, census information, and the overall climate for business development.

South Africa is located at the southernmost part of the African continent, between the Indian Ocean in the east and the Atlantic Ocean in the west. Its total area is 1,219,090 sq km, with much of the surface making the Kalahari basin.

Official Name: Republiek van Suid-Afrika or the Republic of South Africa

Current President: Cyril Ramaphosa

Total Geographical Area: 1,219,090 kilometers

Population: 51,770,560 (in 2011)

Population Density: 42.4/km2

Capital Cities: Each branch of government has its own capital city:

Cape Town – Legislative

Pretoria – Executive

Bloemfontein - Judicial

Official Languages: Xhosa, Zulu, Afrikaans, Sotho, Pedi, Tswana, Tsonga, Swati/Swazi, Venda, Ndebele and English

Currency: ZAR – the South African Rand

Gross Domestic Product estimate from 2015: in US dollars

Per Capita = $7575.24

Per Capita PPP= $12389.96

Time Zone: UTC+2

Calling Code: +27

Population: Black = 75.2%; White = 13.6%; Colored = 8.6%; Indian = 2.6%

Most people know that South Africa has a vibrant yet violent and racist history through the practice of apartheid that was in place from 1948 to 1991.

Though this system was abolished and South Africa saw its first black president in Nelson Mandela, the legacy of apartheid remains. It will not inhibit your endeavor to start a business in South Africa, but it is good to know that the country of today was shaped by the Apartheid.

South Africa's Geography

South Africa is located on the southern tip of Africa with the Atlantic Ocean on one side and the Indian Ocean on the other. The total land mass includes the Prince Edward Islands as well as the mainland and equals 1,219,090 sq km. The coast line of the mainland alone is over 2,500 km.

Moving in from the coastline one will discover a cast plateau surrounded by the Great Escarpment, featuring the Drakensberg which is its highest point. A large portion of the interior is distinguished by the plains of the Great Karoo, the Kalahari Desert and the commercial farmlands of the Highveld. Below this you will find the Bushveld and lowlands of Limpopo/Lowveld.

South Africa's Religion and Culture

By most accounts, South Africa is a primarily Christian nation with about 80% of the population regarding themselves as such. Protestant congregations are in the majority with Roman Catholics in the minority. Protestant groups include the Zion Christians, the Pentecostals, Methodists, Dutch Reformed, Anglican and non-denominational. The remaining 20% are Muslim (1.5%), Hindu, Jewish, Traditional African and no religious affiliation.

South Africa's multicultural diversity is one of its greatest assets. In majority, we've got the Black South Africans with the most broadly known culture (The beauty and particularity of their art work, dance and music, all influenced by their history, has been acclaimed all around the world). They account for about

75.2% of the population. Among this population, there are diverse ethnic groups and languages. The Zulu and Xhosa speakers are the largest groups.

Then we've got the Afrikaans (Dutch settlers descendants), the English speakers (Descendants of the British colonists) and Indians (Brought by the French Huguenots, Germans and Portuguese), all forming this amazing colorful diversity we have in South Africa today. This all gave the country its title, Rainbow Nation.

South Africa's Climate

The climate has an impact on the economics of the country, and especially depending on where you are located. Much of the country is temperate due to the oceans around it, the northern elevation in the interior, and its presence in the Southern Hemisphere. There are however many zones ranging from subtropical to desert.

In the far southeastern end of the country you will find hot, dry summers and wet winters. This is also one of the windiest areas of the earth year round.

The high plateau of the Free State is flushed with rainfall and few subtropical heat waves. The winters in Johannesburg are dry and cold. The Prince Edwards Islands have the coldest temperatures in the country.

South Africa's Economy

With a fascinating and vibrant history, South Africa offers a vast mix of cultures, languages and peoples. English is the language of the economic, governmental and commercial life of the country. The constitution of South Africa recognizes 11 different languages. This mix of languages and cultures reflects that dynamic of the country.

You will find the most active economic developments in the five prominent commercial centers of Pretoria, Johannesburg, Durban, Port Elizabeth, and Cape Town.

In areas where the devastation of Apartheid was greatest, the toll is still being paid with high black unemployment rates and uneven pay scales. But even in these areas, there is growth occurring due to the policies put in place since 2004 to increase black wealth and entrepreneurship. In the hardest hit areas from Plettenberg to Cape West Coast and Kwa-Zulu Natal North Coast, economic growth is beginning to take hold and new endeavors are springing up every day.

The world of international sports arrived in South Africa in 2010 for a very successful FIFA World Cup and the hope that many other such events will follow.

With its position as the second largest economy on the continent and the 34th largest in the world, South Africa is seen today as a significant player in international affairs and even more so in regional African affairs.

CHAPTER 2

THRIVING SECTORS FOR INVESTMENT AND BUSINESS OPPORTUNITIES

For many centuries, mining has been at the center of the South African economy. The economy has been sustained by this industry, due to the abundance of resources in minerals such as gold, diamonds and silver. Even though mining is still going strong, there has been significant diversification in recent years.

The most successful businesses and a fairly large portion of the South African economy were controlled, for many years, by family businesses both big and small. Those that have succeeded and lasted are in the areas of retail, luxury goods, banking, agriculture and construction.

Mining and tourism were more or less controlled by the government and larger corporations. But now, there are openings in these lines of businesses as well. The economy has seen tremendous growth in: agriculture, technology, tourism, finances, education, E-commerce and manufacturing.

Mining Industry

South Africa's land is a treasure trove of every precious metal, stones and minerals known to mankind. Some are only trace minerals while others include large quantities of great value. The process of digging for precious metals dates as far back as 250BC for iron oxide deposits. They also quarried red ochre for rituals and cosmetics.

Modern mining began around 1852 in the Namaqualand region of the Northern Cape and was focused on digging for copper. Most of this area is now a tourist hot spot as mining has all but ceased. In the late 1860's diamonds were discovered on the Northern Cape and the real mining boom for South Africa began, and continues to this day. This is another tourist hot spot, developed at the site of the Big Hole, which is now a South African icon. The site was in operation from 1871 to 1914, with a production record of 14.5 million carats of diamonds.

Towards the end of 1870, gold was discovered in Eersteling at Pilgrim's Rest and Barberton. One third of the world's gold stock is sourced from mines in the Witwater Basin. This area had 53 mines at its peak operating period in 1970, when 1147 tons of gold were mined.

The importance of gold and diamonds in the growth and history of South Africa is undeniable. Yet, the modern urbanized and industrialized nation owes its success to coal and iron ore mining.

Today's metal of choice is platinum, which was discovered in 1924 and began to grow significantly in the 1970's. Today's mining includes vanadium, uranium, chromium and manganese. South Africa's mining industry is diverse and very important to the rest of the world.

Mining in South Africa today accounts for 4.9% of the GDP and represents the world's largest production of platinum and gold, with coal a close second. 40% of the world's known resources and 10% of the world's gold are found in South Africa. Investing in minerals and South African mines can be a very lucrative business. And there are still possibilities for the discovery of new places to mine for a variety of metals and minerals in the hills of South Africa.

Travel and Tourism Sector

Tourism is a major industry in South Africa. The picturesque beauty, splendid outdoors, sunny climate, fabulous infrastructure, cultural diversity and repute for providing value for money have made it one of the world's fastest growing vacation and business destination.

The direct contribution of Travel & Tourism to the GDP was ZAR113.4bn (3.0% of total GDP) in 2014, with a total contribution of ZAR357.0bn (9.4% of GDP).

Still in 2014, Travel & Tourism directly supported 679,500 jobs (4.5% of total employment). The sector's total contribution to employment, including jobs indirectly supported by the industry, was 9.9% of total employment (1,497,500 jobs).

Most visitors to South Africa come from the African continent itself. The majority are tourists and the rest come in for business purposes.

Perhaps the fastest growing industry on the continent, and particularly in South Africa, tourism attracts more foreign investment and franchising than any other business.

There's a multitude of opportunities in the tourism industry in South Africa. Much of the preparation and legwork can now be done online including e-visas and e-passports.

Urbanization is a lead indicator for growth in the tourism and air traffic industries. By 2030, it is expected that 60% of the population of the world will be living in cities. New cities across the globe are springing up to accommodate this move, and this is true in South Africa as well.

Urbanites have more money, more access to air travel and a mass transportation infrastructure which make tourism more feasible. The people moving to the cities constitute a rapidly rising middle class with the resources and desire to pursue tourism.

The challenge for the future of tourism revolves around meeting the needs of the younger, 24/7-connected generation and at the same time appealing to the ageing, less-connected generation. As we move more and more into the digital age, there will be both opportunities and risks for those in the tourism industry in South Africa. So when considering tourism as a new business venture, it is important to be in touch with both of these segments of the population.

Eco Tourism

South Africa stresses on eco-tourism, or a way of promoting and hosting tourism without harming the biodiversity of the country and the other sectors of the economy. One such example is the establishment of photographic safaris as opposed to big game hunting safaris. Local and regional planning and management are essential to the success of eco-tourism.

Another benefit of eco-tourism is, the cultural heritage of the country is maintained, conserved and respected. The local population is always involved in some way in the planning, developing and maintaining of the eco-tourism business. This is what makes it different from sustainable tourism.

There are non-profit groups that are also heavily involved with eco-tourism. For example, the privately funded Conservation Corporation Africa (CCA), which is the leading African Safari company, operates throughout the continent of Africa. This Corporation uses its profits to fund schools, prenatal facilities, and HIV/Awareness Foundations.

Education Sector

The Apartheid certainly took a toll on education in the country. But today, South Africa makes a great expenditure in education for all South Africans.

The South African system of education today includes primary, high school and tertiary classes. Grade R is a pre-primary year, with Primary going up to grade 7 and high school up to grade 12.

The Department of Basic Education and the Department of Higher Education and Training are the two governmental bodies that oversee primary and secondary schools, along with tertiary and vocational.

The Department of Basic Education (DBE) is responsible for both public and private schools, Early Childhood Development (ECD) and special needs centers. The Department of Higher Education and Training (DHET) is responsible for colleges (FET – Further Education and Training), Higher Education (HE) and Adult Basic Education and Training (ABET).

The public universities, such as the University of South Africa, can be one of three types – traditional, technological and comprehensive. There is a total of 23 public educational institutions in South Africa with 11 traditional, 8 technological and 7 comprehensives.

It is estimated that 7% of the GDP is spent on public education with about 1.4 million higher education students in public facilities receiving financial aid. The government spends more on the educational sector than any other sector. However, the private sector offers more opportunities for investment and is more profitable.

Agricultural Sector

There is a large number of farming regions in South Africa, separated by climate, soil type, vegetation and farming methods. The agricultural sector of the South African economy is divided into two major sections, traditional and commercial, sometimes referred to as subsistence and commercial.

Subsistence or traditional farmers produce just enough crops to feed their families and their animals. These farmers make little if any income from their crops.

Commercial farmers run large-scale businesses that produce crops for wholesale or sell directly to retail outlets. This is income-based farming. These farmers feed a large portion of South Africa, the African continent and the Western world. South Africa is a leader in exported food worldwide.

1.2 million square miles are set aside for agriculture, creating ample opportunity for businesses. The diverse climate throughout the country results in a wide variety of crops. South Africa's diverse topography enables the country to successfully produce crops on 17% of the land, with 22% considered high potential arable land. There are seven such regions developed throughout the country, from desert, to sub-tropical, to Mediterranean.

The main issue with farming is the lack of water and irrigation. Over half of all the water in the country is used in agriculture. There is a concern that the water supply is decreasing and could be reduced by as much as 60% in the next 50 years around the Western Cape. Climate change and land mismanagement by government and farmers have led to negative impacts on crops, especially maize.

When considering this field for investment, the most profitable products include: wheat, citrus fruits, wine, sunflowers, sugar cane, maize and flowers. South Africa produces more chicory root than 96% of the world. This is also true of grapefruit and cereal grains. The South African dairy industry produces a tremendous number of products and provides full time employment for 60,000 residents and contributes financially to 40,000 more.

Financial Banking Sector

The financial sector is one of the most sophisticated aspects of the South African economy. Both local and foreign investors have found profitable niches within commercial, merchant and retail banking.

The primary players include the South African Reserve Bank and a few larger and mid-sized banks. There are also several foreign banks currently operating in South Africa. The major financial institutions include: Absa Bank; FNB; Standard Bank; Nedbank; FirstRand ltd

Regulation and Legislation

In any financial market, the regulatory and legislative environment plays a major role. Two pieces of legislation govern the financial sector in South Africa, the Banks Act of 1990 and the Mutual Banks Act of 1993. This legislation set up the Reserve Bank of South Africa, which was tasked with the registration of banks and mutual banks, as well as overseeing the enforcement of the regulations and requirements found in both laws.

Financial Non-Banking Sector

The South African Financial Services Board (FSB) is not tied to the government or the banks. It regulates markets and other financial institutions, such as brokers, insurance agencies, and fund managers.

It is joined in the regulation of credit and debt counselors by the National Credit Regulator for enforcement of the National Credit Act. This legislation is geared toward making credit more available, especially for the economically marginalized in South Africa.

Then there is the stock exchange – a very good way to get started in business in South Africa. The Johannesburg Stock Exchange is the world's 17th largest Stock Exchange. There are over 900 securities and about 400 businesses listed on this exchange, making it larger than the Singapore and Moscow exchanges, and the largest on the continent. The JSE (Johannesburg Stock Exchange) offers users and brokers some of the most cutting edge technology in the world, including infrastructure and first class surveillance systems.

Joining with Russia, Hong Kong, Brazil, India and China in 2011, JSE became a founding member of the BRICS Exchanges Alliance. JSE also runs an alternative board known as Altx or Alternative Exchange. This board represents a starting place for those new to South African business as it serves small, new and growing businesses and helps them to raise capital. There are over 100 companies on the Altx board.

Automotive Industry

South Africa's automotive industry plays a key role in the manufacture and export of cars and their components. This industry is used by major corporations for components and to assemble vehicles for the local and global markets.

The automotive and components industry is well placed for investment opportunities. Vehicle manufacturers such as BMW, Ford (incorporating Mazda), General Motors, Mercedes Benz, Nissan, Renault, Toyota and Volkswagen have production plants in South Africa. Component manufacturers such as Arvin Exhaust, Bloxwitch, Corning and Senior Flexonics, also have established production bases.

The industry is largely located in two provinces, the Eastern Cape (coastal) and Gauteng (inland). The most important benefits for these companies are the low production costs and the access to new markets as a result of trade agreements with the European Union and the Southern African Development Community free trade area.

The biggest opportunities can be found in the production of materials such as automotive steel and components.

ICT and Electronics

South African's ICT sector is the most advanced in Africa. The industry is predominantly developed in mobile software and electronic banking services.

These software developers are very innovative and cost effective. So not only do they export successfully to the rest of the world, they are also supported by local organizations and the government. The Industrial Development Corporation, which aims to promote technology development. And the Support Programme for Industrial Innovation (SPII) also provide financial assistance.

The government recently revised the Income Tax Act to encourage inventions and create jobs. Software developers can now claim back 150% of research and development (R&D) expenses.

South Africa is one of the best international location for software development outsourcing destinations and an ideal test lab for innovations. This is due to its diversity of the local market, world class know-how in business and a developing country environment.

Numerous international corporations, have branches in South Africa: Dell, IBM, Unisys, Novell, Microsoft, Intel, Compact and Systems Application Protocol (SAP).

Here are a few investment opportunities:

- The roll-out of wireless networks and technologies and the local assembly of green-energy technologies for electronic components and subassemblies,

- The development of access-control systems and security equipment,

- Automotive electronic subsystems,

- Systems and software development in the banking and financial services sector,

- Silicon processing for fibre optics,

- Integrated circuits and solar cells,

- Export of hardware and associated services, as well as software and peripherals.

Export growth and internationalisation of the country's companies is supported by the Department of Trade and Industry via the Electrotechnical Export Council (SAEEC).

CHAPTER 3

FRANCHISE OPPORTUNITIES

Franchising is always an option for starting up a business anywhere and it is the same in South Africa. However, there are many opportunities and challenges associated with purchasing a franchise. Entrepreneurs wishing to move fast and those looking for a little less risk than a private start-up offers, are drawn to the turnkey situation with a franchise.

When buying into a franchise you are getting an established brand, corporate training, business support and supplies, as well as marketing and advertising programs. Almost any type of business can offer an opportunity for franchising, but you still need to do the work, understand the laws and regulations surrounding franchising, and evaluate the various franchise opportunities available to you.

Steps to Follow Prior to Acquiring a Franchise:

- Find out if you're suited to go into self-employed business

- Research Franchising as an option

- Check your finance availability

- Research and assess the right type of franchise suitable for you

- Visit other franchisees in the brand of your choice

- Conclude legal agreements and finalize funding

Assessment of a Franchise

- Is the franchise profitable now?

- Is the franchisor willing and fast to adapt to changes in the market?

- What type of on-going support will be provided?

- Will you get good training and manuals?

- How long will it take to recoup your investment?

- What is the director's background?

- How successful are other existing franchisees in South Africa and worldwide?

- How many franchises has the franchisor opened in the past 12 months in South Africa?

Indicators of a great Franchise

- **The Brand:** Although a big brand name does not guarantee immediate success, it does make things easier with investors, who tend to be more open to financing solid, reputable and established brands. It also makes driving sales less stressful.

- **The Model:** The best franchises are founded on unique concepts (A brilliant idea that meets a need in the market).

- **The Support, Training and Marketing Strategy:** Good franchises have full ongoing support systems and training in place for their franchisees. They must also have an effective marketing plan in place.

- **The Franchisor's Experience:** When seeking for a franchise, it might be best to stay away from concepts that have not been tried yet, or inexperienced franchisors. It is common knowledge that a franchise successfully built, then replicated several times, can be trusted.

- **The Franchisor's Reputation:** Before getting into business with any franchisor, do some background research on them. A Franchisor with good standings is more likely to conduct business in an ethical manner.

- **The Franchise's History:** You might want to avoid Franchises in shaky financial situations and or those with a track record of lawsuits.

- **Happy Franchisees**: Before buying into a franchise, get in touch with existing franchisees and find out if they are satisfied with the way in which their franchise system works. If you sense resentment or dissatisfaction, you might want to move on.

- **Accreditation**: Reputable franchises are accredited by the Franchise Association of South Africa (FASA) and subscribe to their Code of Ethics and Business Practices.

Legislation and Franchise Agreement

There are 2 pieces of the South African legislation that relate to franchising: The Consumer Protection Act (CPA) and The Competition Act

The CPA protects the rights of franchisees. It states that before a franchisee and franchisor get into business, there must be a Franchise Agreement in place. This is a written document that outlines the terms and conditions for both parties.

This document must contain a clause on:

- The franchisee's right to cancel the agreement by written notice, within ten business days after signing. No cost or penalty can be imposed.

- Intellectual and commercial property matters

- The operational details

- The Financial arrangements

- The initial and ongoing rights and obligations of franchisor and franchisee respectively.

This document will also include:

- **A secrecy undertaking**: Document protecting the franchisors' legitimate interests and obliges the franchisee to respect the confidentiality of the information included in the disclosure document.

- **A disclosure document** – This document provides the franchisee, with all the necessary details and financial information about the franchise offer.

- **An operations manual** –Guidelines the franchisee agrees to follow.

- **Lease agreement over premises** – this includes details about site selection and lease negotiations.

Existing Franchises in South Africa

Franchises in SA can be put in different categories: Automotive, Beauty, Financial Services, Fast food restaurants, Restaurants, Real Estate, Security, Tourism, Education & Training, Retail, construction, Cleaning, IT and many more.

Here are a few of the top franchises:

- International Franchises: Domino's pizza, cash converters, subway, KFC, Spar, Wimpy, MacDonald's and Kumon

- National franchises: Steers, Debonairs, Mugg and Bean, Nando's and Keg,

Few Final Points

Research: Franchising is not only for fast food restaurants. Different types of businesses can be franchised. Before buying into a franchise, it is important to investigate into the financial make-up of the business; how much of a contribution will you be required to make, in order for you to buy in? How much debt are you allowed to carry? Do your skills match those needed to run this franchise?

Expectations: You could find out from other franchise owners in South Africa, within that same company, what to expect from corporate in terms of support and success. They should provide: The operating system and administrative system that all franchises use, an operation manual, marketing and advertising support, training of yourself and perhaps some of your staff.

Considerations: Analyze the financial situation of the Parent company. Ensure you can afford the costs required. Make sure the location of the franchise sets you up for success. Be sure to explore all the legal matters involved before signing any document. Meticulously read the franchise agreement before signing.

Finances: Becoming the owner of a good franchise doesn't come cheap. Investing in a franchise depends on the industry and size. It will be wise to look around for business opportunities that match the finances at your disposal. Opportunities in South Africa generally range between R40 000 and R200 000 or more.

Franchising vs. Business Start-Ups: The main difference between starting your own company and buying into a turnkey franchise will be the control. You own a franchise, not the brand, the building or the marketing. The franchisor holds onto these and maintains control.

It takes patience and cooperation to be a successful franchise owner, whether in South Africa or anywhere in the world. It also takes good management skills as well as the ability to network with other owners and members of the community. Sales and marketing skills are needed as well as the ability to pay attention to detail.

CHAPTER 4
START-UP OPPORTUNITIES

Beside the Thriving Sectors for investment and business opportunities discussed in chapter 2, there are many more sectors, maybe on a smaller scale, that could welcome your start-up.

The sectors previously listed and the few ones we are about to discuss in this chapter are just ideas for those not quite sure of where or what to invest into, or simply need more information. Whatever the case, South Africa is not only a continually growing market, full of diversity and opportunities, but also very open and welcoming of new and innovative ideas. So even if your start-up is something new to the market, be bold, study your target clients and get in there!

So, how does one go about establishing a new business in South Africa? Here are a few tools and resources that can help you.

Business Incubators

There are quite a few in South Africa. For example:

- The **Springlab** is a technology Incubator located in Cape Town. It is a good place to begin, if you wish to start a technology company. They can offer you advice and support.

- Also in Cape Town, **88mph** assists mobile-based web startups targeting African markets. They have facilities in Nairobi and Lagos.

- The **Innovation Hub** in biosciences and energy, gives access to other entrepreneurs and innovators, whose experience you can call on.

- The **Cube WorkSpace** and **OPEN**, both offer creative networking spaces for startups in Johannesburg and Cape Town.

- The **Impact Hub** has sites in Johannesburg and across the world. Members of the hub can call on the knowledge and experience of thousands of worldwide members.

Mentors and Business Networking

Here are a few institutions that can be helpful:

- **The Small Enterprise Development Agency (SEDA)**: It was established by the South African Department of Small Business Development, to put new businesses in contact with business advisors and seminars.

- **The Business Skills for South Africa (BSSA):** It is a non-governmental, non-profit organization, with a mission to provide training to new business owners. This is done by pairing the experienced business owner with the new entrepreneur.

- **The Saber Network:** It brings experienced professionals together with new entrepreneurs to offer advice, share experiences, consultation and mentoring services.

Business Accelerators in South Africa are designed to determine what new businesses have the most potential to succeed and provide them with every resource and all the support they need to succeed. This might include capital investments, mentoring sessions, and intensive training.

- **ALN Ventures**'s mission is to help accelerate the growth of the startup, through the early stages of development. They give new business owners access to the African Leadership Network. The goal is to show new business owners how to grow their businesses, rather than spending all their time 'running' it.

- For technology startups, a joint venture between **88mph** and the accelerator program **Umbono** was developed by Google. Their goal is to provide the startups with seed money, workspace, networking support and visibility to investors.

Although capital or access to investors is one of the toughest challenges a new business will face, most support, mentoring and networking organizations can not directly offer such services.

- The **South African Department of Trade and Industry** offers grants to small businesses in order to get their project up and running.

- The **Small Enterprise Finance Agency (SBFA)** gathers funding from a variety of sources for small to medium-size businesses throughout South Africa.

- Then there are **Crowd Funding sites** specifically for new South African enterprises. StartMe is an example. They are more successful when it comes to launching products.

Lucrative Startup Ideas

South Africa has been a welcoming economy with a solid entrepreneurial environment for many years. The country offers both the natural and financial resources that allow entrepreneurs to flourish. By starting your own business in South Africa, you are able to offer employment to others and add to the wealth of the country, as well as yourself. As you consider starting a business in South Africa, here are a few things you will need to keep in mind:

- Be financially prepared, by ensuring you have enough capital to either purchase the business you want or startup a business from scratch. Consider the costs of startups, materials, operations, marketing, advertising and a contingency fund.

- Understand the field of business you plan to get into.

- If buying an existing business, be sure to do your homework and research the situation. Why is it for sale? What is its current market value and financial situation?

- And if you would like to take extra precaution, you could also use a focus group and/or an investment professional to be sure you are making the right decision.

Work From Home Opportunities

The most lucrative of the work-from-home opportunities include:

- E-commerce Websites – You can pursue this opportunity in a variety of ways. You can use a wholesaler to stock your online store or you can create the items that are sold in your online store. This work-from-home opportunity has become more profitable as South Africans have become more comfortable with online purchasing and its convenience.

- Virtual Assistants – Becoming a virtual assistant and working freelance from home is a great way to start a business. Find just one client to start with and do whatever online services that client needs – data input, report generation, materials ordering, typing and research assistance and many more. Add to your client base until you are working the number of hours you wish to per week.

- Website Consulting – If websites are your passion and you have extensive web development knowledge, your business can center around helping others design and grow their own websites. Write the content and set up the server site. You can also stay a consultant after the site is up and running.

18

- Corporate Catering – if cooking or baking is your passion, start a home catering business. Get in touch with businesses, offer them samples of your food and then pitch providing meals for their conferences and meetings. You can also provide daily lunches and afternoon snacks to corporate business parks or office parks.

Culinary

As mentioned above, a business in the food industry or restauration can be very lucrative. However, you will have to be good at marketing and sales. Whether your goods are savory or sweet, entrees or desserts, you need to market them and yourself to a specific target market selected after thorough research.

Your clients could be local restaurants, businesses that want you to provide their employees meals on a regular basis or simply catering for special events. There are all kinds of opportunities out there, but you will have to go and find them.

Clothing and Textile

There are plenty of resources and raw materials, and the market for South African designed and made clothing is flourishing. Not only do South Africans purchase these types of products, but so do the surrounding African countries. If you have an online store you can sell your finished products anywhere in the world.

Landscaping

A very popular and growing business opportunity, is in the area of both public and private landscaping. As with most businesses, you can begin from scratch or you can purchase an existing landscaping business. And as South Africa's middle and upper classes continue to develop, there will always be more need for landscaping and landscape architects.

The Institute for Landscape Architecture in South Africa (ILASA), is a volunteer organization, registered with the South African Council for the Landscape Architectural Profession. Its mission is to advance the profession of landscape architecture and uphold high standards of professional services to its members; furthermore, to represent the profession of landscape architecture in any matter which may affect the interests of its members.

Pets

As it is around the world, commerce surrounding pets is expanding and growing in South Africa. The more developed a country becomes, the more people have pets and the money to spend on them. In the city of Johannesburg, on any given day, you can spot one or more pet grooming mobiles driving around town. There are pet stores, pet boarders, dog walkers, obedience classes, agility classes and pet sitters, to mention only a few. If you have a passion for animals, then South Africa has a growing market for your business.

Real Estate

Investing in South Africa's real estate is booming at the moment. Since there are no restrictions on foreigners purchasing property in South Africa, many are flocking to do so. So getting into real estate now may be a smart business move.

However, It's important to know the laws before jumping in:

- Find a knowledgeable professional to lead you through the sophisticated freehold and leasehold land registration.

- Know if you are buying the home and the land or just the home.

- Make sure you understand the conveyance fees you have to pay when the title is transferred on the property.

- If you are buying a property to develop or mine it, you should know that just because foreign nationals can purchase land doesn't mean they own the minerals in the land or can improve the land without additional permissions.

- Finally, it is important to learn the protections and restrictions that the South African government has placed on some land areas in recognition of tribal rights. It is important to know if the land you want to purchase is in a protected area. Be sure you use a professional to represent your interests in this sale.

So, as you consider developing a Startup in South Africa, it's important to consider the economic situation in the region where you will be creating your business. It is best to center your business in an area that's already showing economic growth and stability.

CHAPTER 5

STEP BY STEP: HOW TO REGISTER YOUR BUSINESS

Before considering a business in South Africa, there are some very important aspects you must put into consideration. One of them is how to go about setting up and registering a new business.

There is a legal and fairly bureaucratic procedure you will need to go through when registering a new business. The Companies and Intellectual Property Commission (CIPC) has authority over all new firms, so you will have to register with them. There's a variety of ways in which you can go about this, but the information needed and process to follow is the same.

To register your business, you will have to:

- Complete an online registration with the CIPC

- Open an account with the agency BANK.

- Register with the South African Revenue Service (SARS) for income and withholding taxes, (PAYE or pay as you earn), SDLR (Skills Development Levy Registration), and UIF (Unemployment Insurance Fund).

And for some businesses:

- Register for VAT (Value Added Tax) at SARS

No matter how you register, there will be a registration fee that will range between R125 and R475. And a R50 cost for each name reservation application.

Registering with the CIPC

Go to www.cipc.co.za. This process will require you to provide:

1) Owners and Directors

- Owners/directors names

- Country of origin

- ID/Passport Number

- Dates appointed as owners/directors

- Date of birth for owners/directors

- Owners/directors phone and email

- Owners/directors address and postal code

2) Company Information

- Year end and annual Financial Reports

- Authorized ownership shares

- Website address, email address, physical address and postal code

3) Reservation of Company Name

You need to know what you want your company's name to be and reserve it through this process. You could either use a pre-approved name or select a new name. In the latter case, you will be required to provide several other options as your first choice might already be taken. This process can take between 3-5 days.

4) Request for Additional Documentation

Following your reservation of the company name, an email will be sent, asking for additional documentation. Some of the documents you will be asked for include:

- Certified copies of the ID documents of all directors and owners.

- Certified ID copy of the person making the application, if applicant is not listed as one of the directors and owners indicated above.

- Signed registration forms.

Opening a Business Bank Account.

You will have to go to an Agency BANK. Having all your documents in order is essential before you approach any bank. If you have all your documentation ready, this process will only take about 24-48 hours. The documents required are:

- Proof of identity for all the directors and owners.

- The original founding documents for your company.

- Deposit of about 175 SAR (Each bank has a different fee structure, so shop around).

Registering with the SARS (South African Registry Service)

This involves registering for income tax and withholding taxes: Pay As You Earn (PAYE), Unemployment Insurance Fund (UIF), and Skills Development Levy Registration (SDLR)). You will need to provide:

1) Income Tax registration

- Proof of identity of all the owners and directors.

- Registration Certificate.

- Bank Statements.

2) PAYE, UIF, SDL and SDL registration

- Submit the EMP 101e form, available at the local SARS office or online. Registration is immediate.

VAT Registration

This is the Value Added Tax, that is added to goods and services in South Africa. Items removed from the country with a value of more than R250 may be eligible for a refund. A claim for the refund must be made with the South African Customs Authority.

You will need to provide:

- 101 VAT application form completed and signed.

- Company Tax Number

- Certified copies of registration documents. These are COR 14.1, COR 14.1A, COR 14.3 and COR 15.1A.

- Certified copies of ID documents for the two main directors.

- Original (no printout or photocopy) signed and stamped bank letter confirming the business bank details.

- Original proof of recent business municipal account

- Recent original residential municipal account of the individual or representative employer.

- Certification of ID documents for the representative employer.

- Certified copy of signed property lease agreement.

- Completed and signed confirmation of residential address –Form CRA01, available on SARS website.

- Bank statements showing deposits and invoices for the past 3 months.

Non-South African Entrepreneurs

Non-South African entrepreneurs can register a Company in South Africa from outside the country under these requirements:

- **Valid Passport:** The certified copy will have to be in English.

- **Valid Address:** All registered Companies in South Africa need a physical address in South Africa. If you do not have one, virtual Offices are available at www.regus.co.za.

- **Online Registration:** If you are not currently in South Africa, CIPC has an online registration process.

For foreigners who wish to open a Business Bank Account, your physical presence might be required.

- Documents of your Registered Company: In order for you to be able to apply for a business Bank Account, you will need to have a company already registered.

- VISA Document: A certified copy of your VISA (Valid Work Permit or Business Permit)

- Passport: An English certified copy of your valid Passport or Refugee Document.

- Proof of Business Operating Address: A Municipal Account for light/water, or a Copy of a Lease Agreement where your Business operates from, or a Virtual Office.

- Share Certificates: This is a legal binding document indicating ownership of a company and is signed by the shareholders of the company.

Even as you work your way through one or more of these processes in order to register a new business in South Africa, you must follow the Companies Act of 2008. This entire process can take from three to six weeks. If you are the only employee there is less paperwork to fill out. But if you are an employer, you must comply with the Labor Legislation that is designed to protect the worker.

If you feel you will need assistance to get through this process, you could always get the services of a lawyer, insurance specialist, accountant, or hire a Registration Solution Service.

CHAPTER 6
TIPS AND ADVICE

There is always some risk associated with a new business, no matter where you are. So here are a few more tips and advice to help you, as you set about designing your new business:

Checklist questionnaire:

- What type of business (and in what industry) are you hoping to invest?

- What is your target market audience?

- What size company?

- Will you be handling the business on site or from abroad?

- Will your business require employees?

- Will your business require a physical location/venue?

- Are you creating this business as a foreigner or as a citizen of the country?

- Are you familiar with the country?

- Is your business a new concept that will need to be introduced to the people?

- Will you be running the day-to-day activities of the business?

- Do you have help/contacts in your country of choice?

- Do you know how much capital will be required to start off?

- What is your capital?

Advise and recommendations:

You can be sure that your idea or business will be successful if you put in the work required:

- Understand who your target audience/market is.

- Locate the area of the country best suited to accommodate your business.

- Connect with people who could be of help.

- Choose the right publicity channels to make yourself and your business known.

- Also, going in with a partner can save you a lot of money and cut the workload considerably. Remember, you don't have to stay in a partnership forever, but it is an easier and quicker way to get started.

- When the country you're going into is foreign to you, it is important to know and understand the people you are going to be offering your services to, the culture, traditions, and ways of doing things.

- Choose your investment sector: The financial sector has different rules from the educational sector, for example, and this will impact the way you set up your business.

- Develop a detailed business plan: It must lay out your specific goals and be sure that they are realistic. While passion and ambition are essential, you must also have specific business objectives and a clear vision as to how to meet those goals.

- Be competent and coherent when it comes to today's technology and processes: This is a vital step, even if your product is not in the high tech or digital field. Some of the means for marketing your products or running your business will be digital, so you need to understand software and digital processes. You must be technologically literate, in order to compete in today's market. Customers will expect no less.

- Know your clients: Make it a point to know as much as possible about your clients and potential clients. Your customers are your business. Without them there is no business. Know and treat them well. Find the best means of communication with your customers.

- Know what you need: Entrants to the South African market might consider working with locally hired representatives to provide guidance on the business environment, identify customers, and obtain market information. For products requiring after-sales service and spare parts, it is recommended that exporters consider operating through a distributor or dealership. Agents and distributors must register with the government and their contracts must be notarized and published in the local press.

Attention

Just as in any other country in the world, corruption does exist in South Africa. It is advised you ensure that you go through the right channels and institutions whilst creating your business.

Should you decide to travel to South Africa, beware of all the visa requirements. Travelers should obtain the latest information on entry requirements from the nearest South African embassy or consulate.

If you are starting a business in South Africa from abroad, ensure you use established companies or reliable contacts to help you register your business and or run your activities.

Finally

Setting up a business in South Africa can be done with relative ease. However, it is not an undertaking that can be taken lightly.

Constantly research market trends and best practices to improve your services and deliverables, then update your business plan to remain a step ahead of the competition.

Resources for Further Research

The organizations and resources listed below were used as reference for or have been partially introduced in this book. Should you need more information or require help to start your business in South Africa or any other African country, please contact us via our website: www.startabusinessinafrica.com email: info@startabusinessinafrica.com or social media Instagram @SABIAFRICA1 and we will be more than happy to assist.

1. WTTC: World Travel & Tourism Council. https://www.wttc.org/-/media/files/reports/economic%20impact%20research/countries%202015/southafrica2015.pdf

2. South Africa: Culture, History and Tourism http://www.southafrica.net/za/en/articles/overview/culture-history

3. Our Africa. http://www.our-africa.org/south-africa/people-culture

4. Trading Economics. http://www.tradingeconomics.com/south-africa/gdp-per-capita

5. IEconomics. http://ieconomics.com/south-africa

6. Which Franchise. http://www.whichfranchise.co.za/franchise-step-by-step-guide/

7. South Africa: Brand South Africa's Information Gateway. http://www.southafrica.info

8. NAAMSA: National Association of Automobile Manufacturers of South Africa. http://www.naamsa.co.za

9. CIPC: Company and Intellectual Property Commission. http://www.cipc.co.za

10. SARS: South African Revenue Service. http://www.sars.gov.za/Pages/default.aspx

11. Regus: Physical and Virtual Workspaces. http://www.regus.co.za

12. SARS: Register for VAT. http://www.sars.gov.za/ClientSegments/Businesses/My-Bus-and-Tax/Pages/Register-and-Deregister-for-VAT.aspx

13. Just Landed: South Africa Guide Property. https://www.justlanded.com/english/South-Africa/South-Africa-Guide/Property

14. STATS SA: Statistics South Africa. http://www.statssa.gov.za

15. Chambers of Mines. http://www.chamberofmines.org.za

16. South African Government: Education. http://www.gov.za/about-Sa/education

17. South African Government: Agriculture. http://www.gov.za/about-sa/agriculture

18. The Banking Association South Africa. http://www.banking.org.za/about-us/association-overview

www.ingramcontent.com/pod-product-compliance
Lightning Source LLC
Chambersburg PA
CBHW031507210526
45463CB00003B/1114